Let's look inside
Pyramids

Created by
Claude Delafosse
and Gallimard Jeunesse
Illustrated by
Sabine Krawczyk

*At the back of this book
you will find a press-out paper torch,
and a pocket to keep it in.*

FIRST DISCOVERY / TORCHLIGHT
MOONLIGHT PUBLISHING

People who explore the past bring light to dark places. What treasures and secrets will we uncover in an Egyptian pyramid?

In this book, you'll marvel at the extraordinary objects and works of art that we'll find.

Thanks to a simple torch made of paper, you can explore the dark pages of this book.
It's like magic!

You'll find the torch on the last page.
Press it out and slide it between the plastic page
and the black page underneath it. You'll be
amazed by what you light up!

In the next room, there are carvings on the walls. The artist has shown Nenuphar sitting down to a feast.

Egyptians believed that people needed food after their death.

Nenuphar would be able to drink from these fine glasses.

As you move it around,
little by little you'll discover
all the details hidden in each picture.

More than 4,000 years ago,
the Egyptians built vast pyramids
and splendid tombs.

Archeologists look for traces
of this wonderful civilisation.

Sometimes they dig for months or years
without finding anything interesting.

But today, these people have found some
steps going downwards into the darkness...

A passage leads
into the hillside.
This must be a tomb!
The walls are covered with
little pictures, or hieroglyphics.
They'll give us the name
of the person buried here.

The
small
figure to
the left
shows
it was
a woman.

To find out her name, look for letters on the right hand page
to match the pictures here. Write them down in the boxes.

V

H

A   O

I   P   W

B   J   Q   X

C   R

             K

D

             L   S   Y

E

                          T

F   Z

             M

                                                         CH

G   N   U

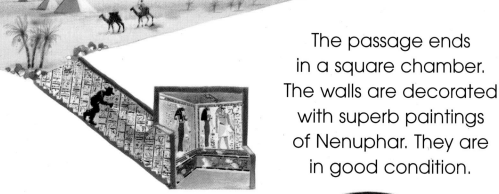

The passage ends in a square chamber. The walls are decorated with superb paintings of Nenuphar. They are in good condition.

The nenuphar is a symbol of rebirth.

The Egyptians used to paint the walls of a person's tomb with pictures of the things they loved in life.

In the next room,
there are carvings
on the walls.
The artist has
shown Nenuphar
sitting down
to a feast.

Egyptians
believed that
people needed
food after
their death.

Nenuphar would
be able to drink
from these fine glasses.

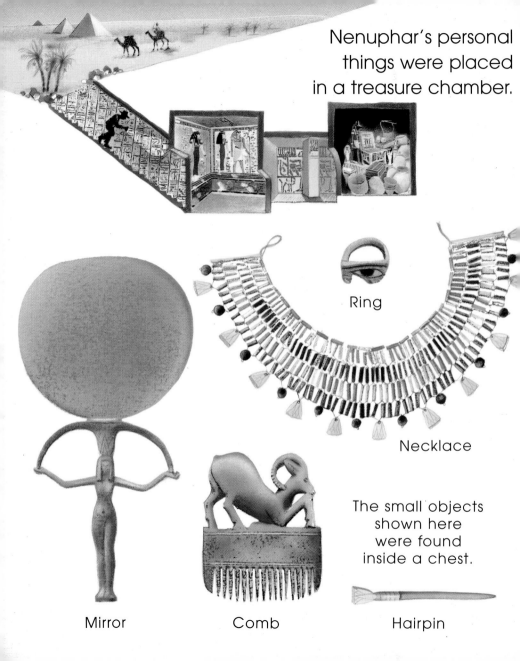

Nenuphar's personal things were placed in a treasure chamber.

Ring

Necklace

The small objects shown here were found inside a chest.

Mirror

Comb

Hairpin

The last room
is the burial chamber.

In the centre of the room
stands the painted coffin.
Inside it is the sarcophagus.

Anubis   Thot   Isis   Horus   Osiris

Paintings of Egyptian gods cover the walls. These gods
were thought to go with a dead person on their last journey.

Egyptians embalmed the body so that it was preserved.

First, water was sprinkled on the body to purify it.

Then the embalmers went to work.

Internal organs were removed and placed in vases.

The body was wrapped in bandages. It was now a mummy.

Many Egyptian treasures
have been brought to museums
where everyone can see them.

Now that you've
explored the dark tomb
in this book, why not
go and look at
real objects in
the light of day!

These details are from the dark pages of the book.

Can you find them using your magic torch?

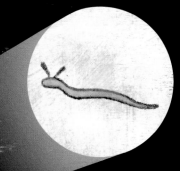

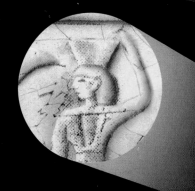

FIRST DISCOVERY
NEARLY 100 TITLES AVAILABLE IN SIX SERIES:

ABOUT ANIMALS
THE EGG
BIRDS
THE OWL
THE EAGLE
DUCKS
PENGUINS
FARM ANIMALS
THE ELEPHANT
WHALES
THE HORSE
MONKEYS & APES
THE BEAVER
BEARS
THE WOLF
DOGS
CATS
THE MOUSE
SMALL ANIMALS IN OUR HOMES
THE LADYBIRD
THE BEE
THE BUTTERFLY
THE FROG
DINOSAURS

ABOUT NATURE
FLOWERS
FRUIT
VEGETABLES
THE TREE
WATER
THE RIVERBANK
UNDER THE GROUND
THE JUNGLE
EARTH AND SKY
THE SEASHORE
WEATHER

ABOUT PEOPLE
COLOURS
COUNTING
UP & DOWN
TIME
LIGHT
PICTURES
SHAPES
MUSIC
CHRISTMAS AND NEW YEAR
PREHISTORIC PEOPLE
PYRAMIDS
HOMES
THE BUILDING SITE
THE TOWN
THE CASTLE
CATHEDRALS
CLOTHES AND COSTUMES
AMERICAN INDIANS
FLYING
ON WHEELS
BOATS
TRAINS
SPORT
FOOTBALL
FIRE-FIGHTING
THE TOOLBOX
THE TELEPHONE
THE STORY OF BREAD
SHOPS
HANDS, FEET AND PAWS
BABIES
THE BODY
HOW THE BODY WORKS

FIRST DISCOVERY / ATLAS
ANIMAL ATLAS
PLANT ATLAS
ATLAS OF COUNTRIES
ATLAS OF PEOPLES
ATLAS OF ANIMALS IN DANGER
ATLAS OF SPACE
ATLAS OF THE EARTH
ATLAS OF CIVILISATIONS
ATLAS OF ISLANDS
ATLAS OF FRANCE

FIRST DISCOVERY / ART
PORTRAITS
LANDSCAPES
ANIMALS
PAINTINGS
LET'S VISIT THE LOUVRE
SCULPTURE
VINCENT VAN GOGH
HENRI MATISSE
PABLO PICASSO

FIRST DISCOVERY / TORCHLIGHT
LET'S LOOK AT DINOSAURS
LET'S LOOK AT INSECTS
LET'S LOOK AT ANIMALS UNDERGROUND
LET'S LOOK AT ANIMALS BY NIGHT
LET'S LOOK AT CASTLES
LET'S LOOK AT THE SKY
LET'S LOOK INSIDE THE BODY
LET'S LOOK INSIDE PYRAMIDS

Translator: Clare Best
ISBN 1 85103 287 8
© 1998 by Editions Gallimard
English text © 1999 by Moonlight Publishing Ltd
First published in the United Kingdom 1999
by Moonlight Publishing Ltd, 36 Stratford Road, London W8
Printed in Italy by Editoriale Lloyd

the most innovative books ever designed for young children

FIRST DISCOVERY

See the magic of the transparent pages transform the pictures!

This well-known series currently includes over 80 titles covering a wide variety of subjects, to delight and captivate children of all ages, starting as young as 5. The original range has recently been complemented by **First Discovery / Art** and **First Discovery Atlas**.

MOONLIGHT PUBLISHING

Flying

N° 20

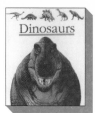

Dinosaurs

N° 21

Homes

N° 22

The Horse

N° 23

The Story of Bread

N°62

Babies

N° 25

Whales

N° 26

Boats

N° 27

Pictures

N° 28

Farm Animals

N° 29

The Riverbank

N° 30

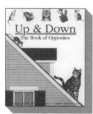

Up & Down
The Book of Opposites

N° 31

Shops

N° 63

Music

N° 33

Monkeys & Apes

N° 34

Light

N° 35

The Bee

N° 36

Clothes & Costumes

N° 37

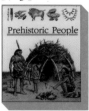

Prehistoric People

N° 60

Time

N° 39

If you would like to order books in the **First Discovery** series, please take the order form overleaf to your Bookseller, who will be happy to supply you.*

In case of difficulty, please send the order form directly to: **First Discovery Mail Order**, 3 Adam & Eve Mews, London W8 6UG Tel: 0171 565 8777 Fax: 0171 565 8779

Signature

Name

Address

Postcode

Tel. No.   Fax No.

Please make cheques payable to: **First Discovery Mail Order**.
I enclose a cheque for

or...

Please debit my Access/Visa/Mastercard/American Express
(delete as appropriate)

Card no:

Expiry Date:

Name on card:

*Booksellers please note
Trade orders to **Ragged Bears Ltd**
Ragged Appleshaw, Andover, Hants. SP11 9HX
Tel: 01264 772269 Fax: 01264 772391
(Cheques made payable to Ragged Bears Ltd)

ORDER FORM

MOONLIGHT

PUBLISHING

Price list:
First Discovery: £6.99
First Discovery / Art: £6.99
First Discovery Atlas: £6.99

For ordering details please see overleaf

TITLE	UNIT PRICE	NUMBER	TOTAL
SUBTOTAL			
POSTAGE & PACKING	FREE IN UK		
TOTAL			

The Beaver

N° 40

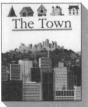

The Town

N° 41

The Toolbox

N° 42

Counting

N° 43

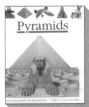

Pyramids

N° 44

The Owl
and other night-flying animals

N° 45

Sport

N° 46

American Indians

N° 47

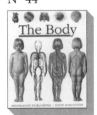

The Body

N° 48

Shapes

N° 49

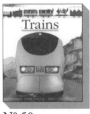

Trains

N° 50

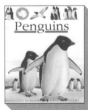

Penguins

N° 51

The Frog

N° 52

The Wolf

N° 53

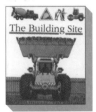

The Building Site

N° 54

The Telephone

N° 55

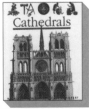

Cathedrals

N° 56

The Butterfly

N° 57

Christmas
and New Year

N° 58

Dogs

N° 59

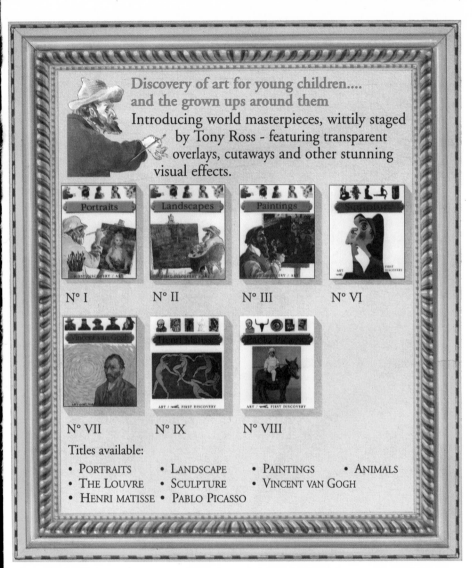

Discovery of art for young children....
and the grown ups around them
Introducing world masterpieces, wittily staged
by Tony Ross - featuring transparent
overlays, cutaways and other stunning
visual effects.

Nᵒ I   Nᵒ II   Nᵒ III   Nᵒ VI

Nᵒ VII   Nᵒ IX   Nᵒ VIII

Titles available:

- PORTRAITS
- THE LOUVRE
- HENRI MATISSE
- LANDSCAPE
- SCULPTURE
- PABLO PICASSO
- PAINTINGS
- VINCENT VAN GOGH
- ANIMALS

FIRST DISCOVERY / ART

FIRST DISCOVERY

The Ladybird
N° 1

Weather
N° 2

Fruit
N° 3

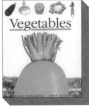
Vegetables
N° 4

The Egg
N° 5

The Tree
N° 6

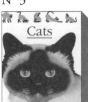 
Cats
N° 7

Colours
N° 8

Birds
N° 9

Under the Ground
N° 10

Earth and Sky
N° 11

The Castle
N° 12

On Wheels
N° 13

Water
N° 14

The Seashore
N° 15

Hands, Feet & Paws
N° 16

How the body works
N° 61

Flowers
N° 18

Bears
N° 19

FIRST DISCOVERY ATLAS

N° A1

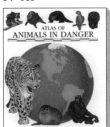

N° A2

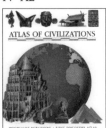

N° A3

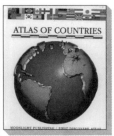

N° A4

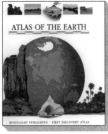

N° A5

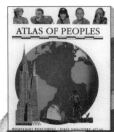

N° A6

N° A7

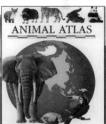

N° A8

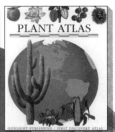

Special effects add to the sense
of discovery

Fact-filled, exquisitely illustrated,
with die-cut surprises and peel-
away fun First Discovery Atlas
encourage young children
to explore the world
around them:
introducing the
five continents,
their peoples,
habitats and
wildlife...